Peter Boyle

&

M.T.C. Cronin

Also by M.T.C. Cronin

Zoetrope – we see us moving
the world beyond the fig
Everything Holy
Mischief-Birds
Bestseller
Talking to Neruda's Questions
My Lover's Back ~ 79 Love Poems
The Confetti Stone and other poems
beautiful, unfinished ~ Parable/Song/Canto/Poem
<More or Less Than> 1-100
The Ridiculous Shape of Longing
    — New & Selected Poems (English/Macedonian)
The Flower, the Thing
Our Life is a Box. / Prayers Without a God
Notebook of Signs
Irrigations (of the Human Heart) ~ fictional essays
    on the poetics of living, art & love
Squeezing Desire Through a Sieve ~ Micro-Essays
    on Judgement & Justice

Also by Peter Boyle

Coming home from the world
The Blue Cloud of Crying
What the Painter Saw in our Faces
Museum of Space
Reading Borges

(as translator)
The Trees: Selected Poems of Eugenio Montejo

HOW DOES A MAN
WHO IS DEAD
REINVENT HIS BODY

?

the belated love poems
of
thean morris caelli

Shearsman Books
Exeter

Published in the United Kingdom in 2009 by
Shearsman Books Ltd
58 Velwell Road
Exeter EX4 4LD

www.shearsman.com

ISBN 978-1-84861-016-3
First Edition

Copyright © M.T.C. Cronin and Peter Boyle, 2009.

The right of M.T.C. Cronin and Peter Boyle to be identified as the authors of this work has been asserted by them in accordance with the Copyrights, Designs and Patents Act of 1988. All rights reserved. No part of this publication may be reproduced, stored in a retrieval system, transmitted in any form or by any means, electronic, mechanical, photocopying, recording or otherwise, without the prior permission of the publisher.

Acknowledgements

(Australian publications unless otherwise indicated.)
Best Australian Poetry 2004 (UQP); *Gutcult* (USA); *Jacket*; *La Traductière* (France, in French translation); *Meanjin; Otoliths; Postwest; Stylus;* and *Southerly*.

HOW DOES A MAN
WHO IS DEAD
REINVENT HIS BODY

?

EPITAFIOS
AFTER LIFE, AFTER DEATH

Had he lived, Thean Morris Caelli would have died. From that death—as from all deaths—poems came. In the Melbourne suburb where he lived, had he lived—with his son and daughter and Irish ancestors from the gallows to the Gold Rush, from the Gold Rush to the Republic, with his small obsessions and incorrigible passions, not forgetting his bountiful inebriation—he loved absolutely. To love this way means to accept the great amount of living that must be done in death.

In his long post-death life it seems he split himself, a natural thing the dead might do to remain in conversation. But maybe a dual voice simply seemed more suited to talk of what it is that joins us, our shared exposure, an expression of any number but that is greater than one. Without doubt, he fragmented and if it were possible to count the true nature of things he would be counted therein.

In the afterlands where he travelled, almost incognito, it was natural for him to encounter other poets. Had he lived in 1890 he would have written letters to Mallarmé and lived in China. In his late 20th Century stumblings he fell into the company of Paul Celan and César Vallejo, their words echoing the crowded glitter of betrayed faces, their stranger-speak bearing the due frivolity and jaggedness to let a world show itself. Thean listened, then wandered further. Flipped cards left in a bar in the afterglow of eighteenth century Madrid became a tarot that wandered to India, all roads intersecting. In a pond in East Anglia he heard, whispered by reeds, the story of a woman who lived in Japan and her sorrow at not seeing ghosts.

Wandering in realms that were vast, or perhaps staying still in a space traversed by many layers, oceans and storms swept across him. Sometimes he spoke in dreams or borrowed dreams or had dreams borrow him, a natural thing to do among the dead where living and dreaming merge into one voice. Indeed dreams and daylight living he considered two languages as intertwined, as necessary to each other as body and breath, as the babble of speech in the quick ear and words that sleep in writing.

The imagined erotic, terrors out of childhood, future hallucinations that being hallucinatory were also real—his poems kept returning to such experiences as they were after all his lived experiences, different, being lived in the multiple dimensions of the afterlands, yet speaking to, unearthing, what might have been the life of anyone.

Contents

Questions the Sea Forgot to Erase   15

Tarots
    Trousers and Shoes   34
    The City of One Thousand Windows   35
    The Spectacle Maker   36
    The Juggler   37
    The Goldsmith   38
    Shadow of a Traveller Found in the Wood
                  Where Oranges Grow   39
    Eggshell Lovers   42
    Sitar Tuner   43

Four Dreams
& a Storm That Began After the Imagination of It   45

Dreambook of the Middle
    Beetle Diaphragm (The Secret of Now)   60
    11 + 7 + 9 is 25 (10 + 9 + 6 is 25)   61
    Oblivion (Night of Nights)   62
    Nets (The Texture of Happiness)   63
    The Collapsing Kingdom (Hiding Out)   64
    In the Dream (In the Dream)   65
    Red Worms (Holy Soldiers)   66
    Instar (Where the Sun is Born)   67
    My Own Dream (Witnessing)   68

To Remain   71

The Summoning Wound
(Book Of Paul Celans & César Vallejos)
    Conversation Beyond the Cloudline   102
    Clothed (César Vallejo)   105
    Open the Chinese Fan, Paul Celan   106
    César Vallejo's Handshake   107

Undrowned	109
César, Well-Dweller	110
The Severed Head	111
Paul Celan and the Pointless	113
Vallejo's Jacket	114
Paul Celan Stepping Out	115
The Poet Vallejo, Announcer of Movement	116
Conversation at the Juncture of the Napo and Ucuyali Rivers, Amazonas	117

OBJECTS OF YOU IN WATER   121

Questions the Sea Forgot to Erase

Which stretches further,
the lines of an open palm
or the one wave the ocean endlessly sends towards us?
How many dimensions intersect in each death?
Tell me,
could you really have held both of me?

The sea opens—
that gravelly sound sucking on tiny pebbles,
your eyes clear, green
like the underside of stones.
From our discarded clothes on the beach
two paths—
one with footprints leading out across the sea,
one going back into doors and spaces,
selves that keep
splitting into other selves. My life
this shared bread your lips give back
moistened. And if I had been strong enough
to carry your fire?

> Like a person I don't know,
> your distance from me
> obsesses me . . .

Like the pebbles.

We argued over dinner
while they sat on a ledge in another room,
already losing their life-colour,
falling like echoes of the beach
when our angry arms swept the afternoon
to the floor.
One of us had brought them home;
the other had seen death in that.

A feather the wind tears, a river that flows on under the ocean,
the owl with its face burned into the window
perched like an infinite yesterday
over the village—
which to prefer, the sadness of permanence
or the sadness of what never happened?
Would we see any better
if we had stayed forever
in the darkness inside a wave?

> Your book, on the chair beside your pillow,
> has fallen open at the last page.
> I try not to see the words
> when reaching over to flick off the lamp.
> Your face twitches
> as the cold rush of dreams pulls you under an ocean
> made of all the lies
> you have ever told yourself.
> If I know the end of a story,
> it is ruined for me—
> a chance that could destroy everything;
> or, the temptation,
> choosing to?

Why does your face tremble into stillness
when a bird crosses your threshold
or your daughter flicks drink
at the faces of the men who watch you?

> Early, when you rose,
> I turned my body, the shape of absence
> bending me to accept those dreams you tossed
> so lightly to the bed.
> In other rooms were children and clocks
> I could hear,

    small voices that played against the walls
    and outside time.

Why does an enormous oak tree blossom under the house?
Does it understand that passion is a language
spoken by the sounds left out of reality?

    How many years we have lived believing
    this house holds what is inside it;
    thinking ourselves
    in some way related to the world.
    I felt passion when you refused me;
    that's the kind of thing I want.
    You felt it only when the body became just
    a body.

The inherited gift of fear
I touch each day
under the ribcage—
can it too make trees blossom?

    I knew you were afraid
    when we talked about having a child.
    Someone we could both imagine—
    and imagine wrong.
    You thought birth was a moment,
    an instant in which you were overwhelmed
    by my strength.
    You said,
    and I laughed, crumpling,
    It looks like a tomato.

If the tomato and the onion could speak,
would life be any different? Would we still prefer to eat what is
stolen?

    As has been written in flowers:
    '. . . What is thrown at you—
    is it free?'

The poet on the balcony, the president martyred in the empty palace,
why was your face forming questions when the world was dismantled?

    Your greatest sadness
    was evident in questions.
    Always suffering and impossibility.
    But which of us comforted the other with this reversal of truth:
    that suffering is the sand trickling from one end
    of the egg-timer which,
    tipped on its head, is joy?
    What is not possible is such a relief.
    I swear the stone won't speak,
    though you listen at the wall of my chest
    for its heaviness . . .

A palm tree, a wave breaking, summer and its imperceptible declensions:
why is a boy walking, his shoulders clenched like deep lessons,
into the steady collapse of the surf?

    Your stories gave me the boy.
    I never met the man
    though I held him in my arms
    and all his children.
    The beach always let us be together,
    an image of paradox when finally we shared
    our separate histories.
    You love water and find nothing to fear
    in leaving the land.
    For me, it was my embarrassed body, the sand
    simply going on forever and the sea full
    of the hands of the dead.

Fishermen spilling squid into the liquid ink-bed of sunlight:
do they count the sandgrains caught in a single eye
or the burn-marks left by nets too hungry for whatever is bottomless?

>Do you remember the evening we slept
>under an upturned boat
>on a narrowing shore?
>A plague of ladybirds came from the ocean
>and filled my cunt, your mouth, our packs
>opened and spilling clothes, passports,
>contraceptives.
>We had gate-crashed a wedding in a cafe
>and eaten chilli prawns without language
>or offering to pay.
>Thousands of kilometres away
>the bugs were still with us.
>I recall looking at your palm and seeing
>a speck of quivering red:
>Put down the lightning you hold
>and be inside me.

In the sweetness of the open hand
why is death the deepest line?

>If you go out, you won't come back.
>If you speak to me, I will hear your last words.
>When I touch your face, I am trying to feel it—
>to create in my hand
>your flesh.
>To want this is like being a ticket-holder
>who doesn't know what the ticket is for.

A harvest of leaves gathered from hills where the birds translate
the verb 'to remain'—
is the best gold the gold of their beaks or the imprint of a tree

growing in your hand
out of all that is fallen?

> I cringe when you throw the children in the air.
> Not because I am afraid you will not catch them
> and the day will become one of those horrible stories,
> but because I begin to desire that they will go up
> and keep going,
> that I will never see their faces
> full of that joyous fright.

When the poet sat down to speak with the birds
did he know that flying would be easier
than asking a single person for truth?

> The cat asleep in the doorway knows
> the truth about flying.

In the old hotel where we made love
is the sky still the same colour—
is the elevator still filled with birds?

> I have written the story you told me
> about your grandfather's death
> and his return as a bird
> to your father's house.
> The cats watched that bird
> and circled it with love.
> It was the only bird that entered the closed garden
> and left with its new life.

A bright summer extends along the line the waves mark—
would your hands slide as easily into mine?
What lies at the back of every mirror?
Is the sea wet enough for you?

    Is your exhaustion only for me?
    You sit so still.
    You sleep so quickly.
    Why don't you think at night
    about our life?

    (My imagination had another woman
    always sharing the bed with us.
    You loved her,
    or at least did not ask her to leave.
    She was young
    and I wanted to see her cry.
    When finally I banished her,
    demanding both your body and your love,
    you insisted she no longer made you hard.
    This, I knew, was coincidence
    for there was some part of your heart
    she had already broken.)

    Living is so easy for you that I can't stop watching.
    I never sleep.

All night the cars wind homeward along the ridge,
the coffee boils in the kitchen—
in dreams, in thoughts
are there names?
What is the one syllable each wave repeats as it splits open?
How far can the dead hold onto a thought?
Tell me your secret name
when you fold inside me like water.

    Listening to the ocean.
    This is a listening that goes on
    and on.
    You begin in childhood

and by adolescence the sound grows louder and louder.
Then, fully grown,
you keep growing, the silence
and its broken tongue
still moaning out there
somewhere beyond this night
and this day.
The sea speaks the final words you hear
before tiredness murders your ears;
the sea whispers a tug
to the water inside you,
pulls your sleeping language to the edge of dreams,
soaks your mouth
and eyes with light.

You knew my name!
It was the repetition, my frankness,
that fooled you into listening
ever harder.
I whisper it now and yet you hear chaos
that has wrestled for itself
a neverending pattern.
An archetype,
not a woman . . .

Our language is stone—
chipped blue icons we fling at each other.
When you pass through a door
haven't you noticed the words
sliding, all jumbled?
Can you speak me
the true word for vanishing?

    The man I left for you
    is still in my dreams

and I am always afraid that I will meet him again
and have to explain the beauty
your love has given me.
I left him my clothes, my furniture, my books.
When I try to remember myself among them,
my body becomes transparent,
my hair fine, like trickling sand.
In dreams he is my husband
and I am happy and then all of a sudden, sad,
without questions.

And then, he is you
and my whole self becomes naked
and I ask: Isn't this better?
And smile.

When the spool of the present stumbles over itself,
spilling black spaces into your everyday room,
do you know what is right or left,
can you say which keys are yours,
which keys you pocketed?

Sometimes I think
there were finite ways for us to be together.
And then I see us, sitting,
heads bent forward in some unknown conversation
and realize I will never hear the words.
How many houses did we build?
At least one!
How many did we live in?
A dozen or more and from the window of one
you threw a chair
and down the stairs of another
I pushed a wardrobe.
We didn't know what meaning we wanted
to give the word 'home'.

On the stone path where she follows you,
always lingering behind in sunlight,
why does your daughter scowl at your heels?
And the trail of your skirt,
how it flicks against the anger of your feet,
and from under the earth
how I long then
to be anything that could touch you,
leaves that fall all over your body,
a doorway's shadow
trembling along your hands—
don't you sometimes feel this?
Don't we each come into the world
with our own strange
measuring cups for the ocean?

> I was never able to tell you what you could tell me;
> could not speak that beautiful language of the world
> you seemed to know so fluently
> whenever you addressed me.
> That sounds formal but its beauty made it so,
> and also so casual—your words seemed to break
> about my body and enter of themselves
> into the openings between my lips,
> my legs . . .

At which moment does the bird between mountains
hear the true pitch of the enfolding music
that calls to it across space—
when lightning carves the pond to splintering ice
or in the long days of the frozen puddle
the moon leaves at the back door
by way of signature?

    I found no relief in silence, mine or yours,
    and as you watched me speak,
    I was growing sick with the tiny phrases
    shut beneath my skin, thickening,
    trapping sweetness.
    I never even said 'I love you'. . .

Can a bucket find the depth of emptiness?
Would it have a fucking clue?

Sometimes I want to take pain
and carve it into my face,
peeling off all the skin.
You who travel from ripeness to ripeness,
can you understand that?

    You feared me and I could see in your eyes the story
    of how women, who do not stab and kill,
    are the keepers of this sentiment;
    how they foster hatred because they love those
    who stab and kill
    and those that are killed.
    You thought I
    was more whole than you . . .

The ocean flowing on under the cold,
flowing under the light,
its waves far and farther out, the few boats riding there, the glide and
dip
of birds tracing distances,
this morning as light washes over my feet on the marble tiles
and the back of the house
is blue with cold and trembling with what has risen for the first time
so early—
the edge of summer—

and what lies under the cold and the light
is immense—
this world here not here that is always shining—
if I seek the salt in your hand
or the warm curve of your breasts
isn't it also that immense space I long to rest in?

> If I rose early, after you, I would see you looking out . . .
> At something.
> And I was looking at you.
> Back in our bed my aching feet found the warm place
> on the mattress.
> I dreamed that the ocean and the land were splitting apart
> inside me; that you were standing in my womb,
> complaining about what you couldn't see.

The rounded pebble, the budding nipple, tender awkwardness of the hair
that hides the sex:
why do you leave all that to invent unhappiness?

> Fucking, I am scared of nowhere.
> We make love even as you walk away.
> The time in the shopping centre
> was the best for me.
> I saw in your eyes then that you have a life like no other.
> The brittle reddish-white of your new beard
> seemed like a snowline—burying
> my lips in coldness.

How does a man who is dead reinvent his body
so it can flutter again in the breeze, enter once more his shoes left at
the door,
sit down and caress the shadows of those he loved?

    I never said it when we lay together,
    but I think you lived our love wearing handcuffs,
    unaware of what they were for.
    You wore a hood
    as if to say to me
    I cannot look at you
    when I could not look at you.
    You tied your words around each other
    until they resembled small fists.

Do doors have names?
Can I open the door to the room
where your whole life blossoms in a glass of stolen water?

    Take me every morning as soon as you wake!
    I need to be pushed.
    If you do not steal all you can from me
    I will keep it.
    Stagnant and stinking.

Does the sea remember each wave
or the garden broom fallen fruit?
Can we have breakfast in the mountains?

    Your back is like a mountain to me.
    I trace my hand up its face and feel longing.
    Is this what it is like to climb?
    Too often I let you turn away
    comforting myself with the belief
    that I cannot think with someone else's thoughts.

Things I never told you.
That night in a dream I was with my brother again—
he wore blue clothes, a blue tie—
he was stepping into a car that was also a boat

moored on the still flat river—
beside it the sprawling house, green fields,
the lushness of a world trapped in its own silence,
and on the other side of the river
what my brother and I would always see—
statues, their faces smashed,
ghosts moving in and out of ruined walls,
disfigured bits of people, what we carried with us
on a river that didn't flow.

How could I tell you that?

Or when everything in me died
and I spent a thousand dollars in two weeks
visiting prostitutes
and had to lie about it, did you believe me?
Holding me in the dark
who do you hold?
At the moments I am closest to you
do you smell my loneliness?
And when I long so much for your breasts
now I am not your husband, now they belong to your daughter
could I really have touched you that day?

> I called out to you.
> The world has arrived again.
> We all recognize it,
> stare at its new face
> that we have never seen before.
> My secret, the one I did not want to give up,
> came to choke me every few years:
> the need to be filled back up
> with someone else.
> I wanted my breasts
> to be like that forever.

Who is the keeper of the honour list
for every emotion?
Why is pain measured in years, joy in seconds?

    Such a short distance, this dance.
    Your hand on my back
    is felt as a hot drunken ache
    in my kidneys, my liver.
    And the world is ending now!
    Even so, can you distinguish
    between your real life
    and everything else?

When the sea first invented the one colour
for love and emptiness,
did it know how perfectly it would fit in a pocket,
how easily it would close in the hand
of a child or a lover?

    (Even noticing most things
    the poet was still suspicious
    of his senses.
    He should have believed the concern of my flesh—
    like words that determine those which come later
    it could have held a special convenience
    for the pieces of himself
    he was trying to fling
    into nothingness.)

How many questions does the sea ask each night,
letting them break over and over
against our dreaming bodies,
taking them back before dawn?
Is the past any closer
than every other mirror?

Pain is not measurable, though we live in a world that counts.
I am meant to know the value of you,
the precise degree of your suffering.

With the tears I catch I am building an ocean
deep only in the present.

I no longer look in my reflection
for the effects of your love on me.

When I swim
the dawn breaks in the small of my back.

TAROTS

TROUSERS AND SHOES

Put some time next to the pit
where the sun is poured to make the bricks of night.
A little grumbling in the ranks
of the self. In grief I no longer understand shoes,
incorrigible, buy shoes anyway.
Perhaps they'll be stolen, perhaps they'll wear—
Out of shadows left in old cups
and too much space between breath
and silence, from the falsehood of floorboards
and hard-won ignorance, I continue—
This means, having a light-green faith in the present
and walking, like the smallest child
in a family, always behind and calling
to the bigger boots, the vanishing shoulders—
I am here, I am here, the years
by my grave are fading like my trousers in the sun.

The City of One Thousand Windows

My love lives in a building made of glass.
When I come to visit
I never know which one of the thousand windows
is hers.
When I say her name
all of them glow with the one inner light,
all of them tremble
as if recognising the sound.
When I take a train to find my love
the doors won't open,
I go round and round the city
and every building has taken something
from her past and her present.
Every ring she gave me I gave to the sea
but I was wedded to her
more deeply than a stone to its sinking.

Where she lives is called a skyscraper
but really it's a failed bridge
as if where we had to go
was out there, the stars
trapped overhead
not shining in our games and in our gestures.

The Spectacle Maker

In the room where you live, my love, below the sea—

In the room where you live you never know how many people
are massacred.

Nine months isn't long enough to learn to breathe—

Nine months I cried once out of happiness
for the pretended banquet.

Worse than blindness is to buy another's eyes—

Worse than bone-dust, the retinas of the new-born child,
expanding and retracting if even you speak.

Open that door which leads you nowhere—

Open the head of the tapeworm and there, glowing, hot,
just your thought and the lion rising from sitting.

In the corner painting straw, the man who made spectacles
for butterflies: what was overwhelmingly visible
flying back to where *it* is found
in the living.

The Juggler

On the fifth night without sleep
when they gave you back the sky
your teeth started hurting—
was Gehenna to be found
in the bills of birds?
Baleful and winking the eye
of your moving hands.

Anonymous, bright, shining
you tossed the world
as if it was the listless
wild plums picked from the tree
which attracts no wind.

'No one can hold your face' you said
as you bedded down
in the space that moved away
from all that would fall.

A crate shatters—the orange rolls towards you.

A house builds itself from old wool.

Two roads step out from the locked door.

Finally, wild from following both
you tempt the numbers from where they rest.
And in the dry bone of your lap—
what you could no longer hold.
And in the open field where you find him—
the juggler with the box of skulls.

The Goldsmith

The chess pieces drop to their death one by one,
they drop with such spirit and intent.

We will not consider dividing says the goldsmith
as if he offers birds that talk a way to live
without revealing their secrets.

He is married to the lantern
whose light may be concealed, silver her eyes
and silver is her breathing.

The element you fear most isn't water
he whispers to her in the barn of straw as the villagers
dance and stain the bucket.

And she blushed black pitch, one by one
patiently threading night into the sky, the sky
into his veins.

The goldsmith with the resting eye,
the goldsmith on the bridge that flows away.

Shadow of a Traveller
Found in the Wood Where Oranges Grow

He goes out to collect the dust.
He goes out to collect the sky.
He savours the raindrops.
He has lived a long time in the stone floor of the house.
He has travelled through stone,
sharing its confusion of distance and space, its hunger for lost
        names.
He enters the spirit of whales.
His veins link him forever with the tracery of leaves injecting their
        shadow into the bitter peel of oranges.
He is quiet as a fish sliced open,
all the bones numbering the generations of his life.

In one of these he was an obstetrician
and counted around him the importance of eggs,
knowing, and keeping the knowledge, that there is a story of zero,
of nothing.

In another he found his fingers
bruised with charcoal and stopped to wonder
if his work was to build fires of warmth
or images.

In his last he entered a tree without a door
and became trapped there, rings of wood marking
each young course he found himself
travelling.

He listened to what might have been
the huge termites of his skull
and heard there was a woman who had found a language
for dreams.

She offered him a mirror with a knife inside it,
an enormous basin filled with stars
that whispered all the secret words
of his childhood.
She said, 'The wind is your true mother.
My breasts can never spare you
the long whirling cycle of pain.
Cup your lips on my sex
that you may travel far
into the skin of countless beings
and know the unbearable throb
of the heartbeat that measures their loneliness.
Understand we are each other's dreams.'

This, if you understand the story so far,
is something he could not wake from
and so it is that we regard someone such as him
as thrashing about in a sleep
that contains all the falling ideas
of a brain too heavy for standing
beside the gate in early morning
watching and waiting to see how the day might stir,
again light and conscious around him.

We go out and put our feet on the stone,
reach and pick the orange already eaten.
It tastes like something that has wedged itself between
the fruit and the idea of the fruit,
interlucent, as if it tasted finally
of nothing but the movement of the air,
highlighted when the leaves exhale softly
towards the future.

And so.
He goes out to collect the dust.

He goes out to collect the sky.
His veins link him forever with the tracery of leaves injecting
 their shadow into the glistening peel of oranges.
Can you identify on your tongue
that sweet bitter shortness?
It is time dissolving.

Eggshell Lovers

They tapped gently at each other.

Shattered like chandeliers in the air of ten centuries.

All they wanted was to float in one shell—

penetrating, not yet touching,

entirely themselves and merged as one,

little specks of cosmic grit

always sticking.

Sitar Tuner

The wood, listening, mellows into time
as it is lived by those dwelling on the sun's surface.
Tightened, the pegs give that long arch
of the lovers' joined breath
where night has no reason to find dawn.
The hourglass, the watercarrier's bell,
the chiming merchant's scale
are muted, taken back from hearing
in these moans, each one of which
clutches you, could free you
into living what you suspect you are.
A vibration masters the fingers, the arm,
that stilled distance of two faces
kissing and drinking in.
What opens in the heart, as it opens,
has no past. Tuning and tuned
inextinguishably
you are.

Four Dreams
& a Storm That Began
After the Imagination of It

'we feel and experience that we are eternal'

dedicated to Benedict de Spinoza

The child shone in the room's centre.
The bed he sat on seemed to carry no weight,
unmarked by shadow.
Again and forever
the moment of the hand letting go,
his head tilted stiffly to one side,
moving back a little way
and a little way
till light and sound stood emptied.

Along the ridgeline
the first winds coming in.
Within it, lost, I go with it,
cradled, racing towards paradise,
the again-and-again instant of birth.

I follow the beginning of the storm
to the point where the island loses the sea
to its subtlety with sky.
Land with no foothold, ocean turning hard
as a split gorge of black rocks.
My ears fill with the weight of night. A persistent ringing—
delicate as Summer shadow over the moan of forest rain—
in a house that might be mine . . .
I tap at the machine to reach you,
Lightning splits this shared black space words cross—

> *All I brought back from my folding through space*
> *is the memory of a book:*
> *its words all numbered sequences—codes*
> *that give birth to monstrous insects of the air*
> *released on the headland in the storm's gathering,*
> *the sky spinning its clumsy arms around me.*
> *They eat the night.*
> *They make the night their bodies*

which wake when the sun touches these old volcanoes
with new fire. The earth
is born in these pages of light . . .

Laughter under the trees, a rowboat setting out
across the narrow wash of waves. Boys
diving from pylons, your mouth touching mine behind
the seclusion of the rocks at the far end of the beach
where the wind died down
depositing the seed.

In a seaside bar the Stranger from the Book called Openings
woke, blinked, pulled down
his dark felt hat that smelt of rain
and saw an enormous map spread out against the wall.
I come from a place called Bitterness, he said,
pointing towards the dotted islands
as cicadas broke free for the first time
from the crippled harvest
as the sun and the moon
slipped forever beyond the carbonised hands of cartographers
and children scooped out of the sand of the dry riverbed
fish who kept burrowing deeper and deeper
in their certitude of ocean.

Decipherment producing
what is deciphered
and whatever it is
like nothing.
Yet still I took my pen and paper and laboured the whole
of my life until it was night and I had labelled
everything.

Bottles of green water washed by generations of sand
shone far below the surface

in the pool the river had hollowed.
Shell collections trembled in their bed
of seagrass and numb thoughtfulness.
And whatever had a name
waited in patience as the unnamed flowed
all around it.

It was after midnight when I watched the oranges
looking back at me. So many years and it comes to this.
The light burns,
you said, speaking softly to me from a photo pegged
among so many others in the uncompleted
mural left behind on the kitchen wall.

There is a dove there. Cliché. Also
the picture of us both laughing that everyone notices. I ask
them why and they say it is because neither of us are even
thinking about love.

Did we think about love?

What bleeds
out of me but words when I speak to you across
the cranes of the city—the skyline is broken everywhere
and I am sure you are still a part of that sleep
I cannot enter: your head, heavy with sand,
your hands pulled by fishing lines
with their hooks far in the mouths
of other dreamers.

You get up.
Once more you turn your back to the window
where night rain is tapping out
blank streaks of darkness.
You take from its shelf the damaged book
and read again the one loose page—

Fragments from the Book called Closure:

'The sun bled out of the narrow room.
We do not see what circles us forever.
The room was growing twilight.
Throughout the house all clocks had been removed.
The door held nothing back.
Inside
only the clothing of a child laid out
for some abolished journey.'

I rearrange the poetry fridge magnets
and on my knees look for lost words
beneath the bench.
So much had died—
in all the trees
moths lived without name or number;
'the old pink-edged cloud of the inhuman'
settled above the canal bank
where the crows were nesting.
So far apart
we read the markings scattered
across each other's eyelids.

Light bleeds. As breath does
in outer space.

Fear surrounds the iron bed. The child floats above
himself—his hands two pale cups
where blood pours.
Frantic whispering at the doorway—
an argument of some sort. The child returns
to his body in order to listen better. Somewhere
his mother, you?, is fretting beyond speech.
A forbidden milky whiteness descends slowly
from the ceiling.

Suddenly everything in the city smelt of urine.

Are we looking for the marks of the dogs? I come across an image
of you reading a newspaper. Men go to war
(so you read)
because their brothers are missing,
and you imaginatively possess their history:
the rain, the fields of dead trees, the snow
in which they searched for the marks
of survivors.

They emptied their pockets and built a small bridge of pebbles.
Explosions happened in the sky. They looked for the date
and found a planet in migration.
Oxygen was on sale everywhere.
Plans were underway for the manufacture of water.

You read from the great Book of Hidden Things:
'No one can be assured of a place in history.'
My feet pushing down water
as if the water had something to say to them—
If this is the sort of thing you read that inspires you
then go ahead.
At the bottom of this is a child who had yet to learn
about air.
People think they can breathe
in all kinds of environments—
without really thinking.

I see your hands making the never sign
and this you do because no one
can hear.

The sound of fans filled the houses of the city
and then the lightning

cancelled all the mistakes of our mouths.
In under ten minutes water filled the kitchen
from gutters wind-clogged with pine needles
and the trees' spiny seeds.
I knew the spot where the refuse gathered and grabbed a chair,
heard you laughing as the flood found its way
to your knees.   'My waters have broken!'
and suddenly I see concrete animals, gathered, pissing
down the drain beneath the perfectly round space
at the centre of a cobweb, gunshot hole
through the sky.
'Why's a fly?' Struggling. Bird whimpering
for its nest.

By morning all the bushes will have lost their flowers
while overhead, the storm, like a rushing plane,
reflects itself as image in the wet earth
of my floor.

> *I was hawking my sidereal roadmaps,*
> *my paintings that were all blank or just*
> *scrawl-marks of lonely fingers,*
> *across the dry oceanbed of the outback,*
> *my face of an elderly Dutch Jew, circa 1670,*
> *versed in scriptures*
> *in the minute perfection of lenses*
> *now hawker, painter and dreamer in this*
> *latest manifestation*
>
>> *'to each form pertains an infinity of manifestations, read*
>> *'modes',*
>> *wherein it persists in acting and being,*
>> *each storm, each lightning flash rippling*
>> *through infinite domains of which we perceive dimly but four'*

> *I parked my ute by the one pub*
> *that stood there on the plain that ached heat and distance*
> *while lightning spoke at the edges of the sky.*
> *My canvasses were stacked in a row in the back of the ute,*
> *bound together, listening to their own silence.*
> *'Imagination', I said, trebling the price,*
> *'has a problem with names.'*

Turning your four faces toward me, again the room in which
I experience the storm: where I learn about something
they call the world through books, where I cannot
learn the world through books; where your
smell is the burning of electric cable
as the printer fuses and your face
the smashed glass of the door
forever opened; tetra-
hedon, your fourth
face—the end

point of my route to you.

Imagination has a problem with waking,
or at least to a state without dreams,
for it asks the dream to keep unfurling across the desert
of wakefulness.
And if I am not to lie forever in beautiful paralysis,
in sleep's resurrection,
will I find who cannot be found in the stone-marked
crevices and erogenous hiding-places
of my own body?

Was our child one of those whose bodies reached
through the dry space of vision
before disappearing gracefully—unexpectedly so,
disproportionate with wild energy—into the sea, slurring

its words beneath a forcing wind? Who
decided on death as the outcome despite facts
and what might exist as their
opposites?

> *A letter fell from between the Book's pages*
> *and burned itself to my ribs*
> *as if a scar in search of skin.*
> *I had been quoting from it—*
> *(it told the story of a friend*
> *in grief's exploratory language:*
> *letters never touching this earth with their feet,*
> *words like rising stars*
> *slipping and turning in the 'mind's eternity'):*
>
> *'How was it I heard the sigh of my child*
> *before he sighed?'*
>
> *'Is prophecy what we give birth to?'*
>
> *Suddenly I could read no more.*
> *A man with arm extended, palm facing me,*
> *fingers pointing towards whatever was above our heads*
> *took charge of the scene.*
> *'Mountains are ideas' he said,*
> *'looking for sea-beds to lie in'*
> *and I turn from him to the hole in the back of my mind.*
> *Paintings from a vocabulary*
> *hang everywhere from invisible ropes*
> *and chains of air—and there you are, beneath the murderous*
> *clouds,*
> *trying again with their great lustre*
> *and disagreeable smell to put forward two versions*
> *of every image:*

*'I will join you such as I am
though in these dimensions
I was sifted the wrong way to be anyone's lover,
my face and hands all ash . . .'*

*Always another sign
and around us an audience
for the writer of echoes.*

'You cannot disagree with this—it's a statistic!'

What I heard I related to error, turning in all directions
towards the sea opening around the island.
All charge me with offences of reason. The indictments pile up.
What was it that stopped me on the headland?
All the way walking back
the coded words of the storm,
some long incomprehensible phrase
seen once in a book, then forgotten,
the book not yet written, a dream or a hope,
something too heavy to carry back into this world.
('Earth' and 'Death' fused
by the transposition of two letters.)

(Daydream)

*Beyond the swirling chaos of the flooded stream
you stepped out on the river's other shore,
a place of white shining emptiness
like a dazzling page that devours
every word set on it.
Before you the bleak sandhills rose, a few
grey-green tufts shaped
like the skeleton of a Question Mark,
crests of white grass, dry winds
that climbed slowly with you*

and, behind you, the river
with its houses, abandoned cars,
uprooted trees, the fridge that floated out to sea
all rushing into the sky's blue curve.
And as you looked forward
you found you were seeing both directions simultaneously,
the transposed image of two worlds
playing against your eyes.
Then you turned as if to come back to us,
as if to enter the river again
and in that moment
your hand held a child you did not see,
our son the size of your waist,
testing the sand with his sneakers,
his gaze on nowhere,
and the one sigh shuddered then
through both our bodies.

When I held your body did my thought come to rest—
inside all turmoil, your wetness, the rush of us both
towards an infinity of otherness—
on the seed that would bruise our hearts
as if a broken rib, an awareness,
a cricket ball tossed at us by a child
from a place beyond his birth?

Coming from so far off
and now having to go back there
all that way,
was the sigh we heard
your way of saying
that nothing had after all changed?

Is what circles us, invisible,
the one thing
we truly are?

May these questions lead a journey through
a gold sky; may they be an earth-
worm jumping its split self
in the arc recognized
by all genes.
No need for some other half, for the bond that forms
between those who share judgement
never dissolves.

The ringing in the darkness
in the house that is mine
as I reach finally
for the phone—

(and if it was truly our child
how I would claw my way across these worm-
threads of space-
time for you,
I, who have neither arms nor a body)

We have lost love, but not how
to stop caring—

(the sky, rounded flecks of meteors the size of all travelling,
green threads of the unborn
tangling together
deep in the river's flood,
trembling under all clearness)

shall we celebrate perspective
with a few words from each of us?

    'lonely, lonely
    we are all here'

Dreambook of the Middle

Beetle Diaphragm (The Secret of Now)

There are circles and they spiral downwards. Inexorably. Tiered layers of an amphitheatre. Delphi perhaps. But also the hillside above the football oval at my old school. Nonchalantly, locked in the agony of making things clear, Dante paces the upper circle with Ezra Pound, shackled in the regulation orange robes of the future, Pound the washed up, the one with the chain of seashells round his neck from his remembered life on the seabed.

The minutes decide who we will make love to. All our appetite is of time. Time and the order of things in it. Thus cruelty sometimes comes before satisfaction and suffering after. Or, in a perfect life, suffering, suffering, then suffering. But it is simply true that you can take a pair of scissors, or a knife, and cut away what you don't want. Such a limp thing as the past can be chopped at the very point where it joins you. The future you can wipe off as if it was steam on the window's pane. As for now? That's what happens when you close your eyes and dream.

I am sixteen. I wake and I am sixty. A tumorous circle like a worm is going down into my head. The bulldozed earth wants to bury me. I cry out towards Pound, 'Mulier muliebris.'

Young? Old? Specifically not. The secret of now is that nothing ever gets closer or further away. You've been in the earth for years waiting for that tiny spider with hands to reach you. Meanwhile, the desert is slowly melting and filling the glass. On the table before you it appears to sleep—just like sand.

What is it you've done? Invited those you admire to drink. Both men make a sign of refusal that suits well the thunderclap. Because you can no longer breathe, because your diaphragm is clicking like a beetle, you turn to them and say, 'There's just no way I'm gonna stand for this death crap.'

11 + 7 + 9 is 25 (10 + 9 + 6 is 25)

Cervantes sat down on the plane beside me as it began to fly backwards to Melbourne. He had just circumnavigated the earth 397 times and was returning from a conference on desertification held in the prosperous and beautifully decorated capital of Antarctica. I asked him what his favourite translation of *Don Quijote* was. 'Oh', he said, 'I planned to write a book by that name but I'm still waiting for a stranger to tell me the best day in the universe to write the first sentence.'

The greatest danger is being dragged back by the raised from the dead. Dragged back to the one long piece of your life, a piece that doesn't work. We are all parched by our inability to drink of life. We deny the earth. We deny ice-bergs. Deny the lighter notes that might balance us between seven and nine. Regardless, to live is best attendance. Sea-sickness and love-sickness are the same. The equation, the curse, is always yourself and all it needs is to be set in motion.

Oblivion (Night of Nights)

He entered a deep room. All the furniture was red. A woman coloured blue drifted across the ceiling laughing. The room was woven from a seamless thread of music—it was *Oblivion* by Hector Piazolla. If you want me, the woman said, you will have to tell me the story of your life. It was then he remembered that he had no name. How can the dead put their lives back together? 'It's in a book', he said, 'It will be in the universal library. Only I can't remember the title or the author.' 'That's easy then', she replied, 'all the dead have the same name.'

This is not being provocative. The animal's throat determines pronunciation. We all know the breeding-place of death. Such a busy nest. Furnished with a platter of fruit, a night of nights, the decimalized cave where all the work gets done. All around it sound castles pave the sky with a shared tree. Fable the accessories. Femininity and masculinity in all their blood and feathers. The canned town. The does. All the poems for Donna. And this all takes place around death which makes no sound.

A maelstrom of silence.

Nets (The Texture of Happiness)

On the beach nets are laid out in rows and a picnic is spread out. Following the urging of the nuns and their threats of violence, I wade reluctantly into the cold waters of the Tasman straits, I and a group of classmates. A wide net is thrown over us. The others know the game and swim rapidly to the sides of the net, slipping out just before it reaches the seabed. It is a very old method of teaching people to be fish. But weights are still strapped to my feet and I can't move fast enough as the net drags me under. Bubbles of lost air splutter around me. Suddenly in the moment of drowning everything changes. The shoreline, the nuns in their black habits, the sun shining steadily in a sky of intense and delicate distances, all glow with a rightness, a clarity, a beauty that has no words. My hands are stroking the still texture of happiness.

There is a life that has nothing in it. It is perfectly empty. Only is such a life, innocent.

The Collapsing Kingdom (Hiding Out)

I was walking in the Cradle Mountain area of Tasmania when I realised I had slipped across the border into Norway. It was one of those everyday platitudes of geography that if you walked far enough south you must always reappear in the extreme north. Norway was filled with refugees fleeing the persecutions, the roaming death squads of Australians. Australia, it was rumoured, had once welcomed refugees fleeing through Norway from the death squads of the Germans. What I remembered most clearly was leaving Melbourne, picking my way carefully along beside the railway tracks, joining my tribal brothers hiding in the scrub, hoping the Australians who wanted to kill us wouldn't find us. One day we were in some mountain passes and I no longer knew whether we were now in Norway hiding from the SS or in Australia hiding from mounted police dedicated to whitening up the country. One morning I found a lone homestead that seemed safe and approached an old man to ask if we were truly in Norway. 'You seem confused', he said, 'there is only one country—its rulers are charismatic criminals who have no interest in geography. It has no borders but everywhere it keeps collapsing into the kingdom of the dead.'

When I was a child I sat with my sister on the beach and watched the slow—yet in sudden movements—crumbling of the monument built entirely of sand. One piece would go and take another whole piece with it. And all the while we were trying to find the way we had arrived here so that we could retrace our steps.

Sometimes when you're lost absolutely enough, a drink appears—champagne?—placed in your hand by an attractive stranger. Someone you know only, but immediately, by their kindness. So with your head bare continue to look for a way home. But remember, the only true direction is a circle. All around it, the dead collapse into life.

In The Dream (In the Dream)

In the dream I slept with the younger brother who never existed of the lover I had before you. The lover before my lover. The imaginary brother in the dream. I trembled in his gaze: open like a palm, exposed to a pure otherness.

In the dream I was a woman and my dress caught everywhere on metal stars strung along a wire. The wire surrounded parts of the dream. Parts from which I was trying to escape. The shredding machine to thread the words out of my voice. The bath that dissolves every wrinkle of my soul so it could be that it never existed.

In the dream I was barren. Left behind. I could hurt no one. Love no one. The only way to describe my presence is with the word 'conscription'. And absence, dangled like a toy on a fish-hook, would be mine to own for ever and ever.

Gradually, I began to understand vengeance. To understand how killing is echoed in killing. How a hammer through the skull could say 'I am'. And when I realized the boy's face, the boy with whom I was naked, I lost history.

Red Worms (Holy Soldiers)

What do I care that the coup master by popular request has reintroduced the pogrom on breathing? I was only here by arbitrary invitation. Escaping up the zigzag of lanes, more worms, sluggish and inspirational, block the route to the summit where a helicopter salvation awaits. Red worms by personal dint. With greyish neck. Like all fates with hearts in another world. Woollen material. Such is my dream. Hurled full of jactation. Dark shark sugar of centuries which break from the jail of time and ally themselves with the jaguar or jade or jaffa of a doorkeeper who drank of jazz and let in the night. You want me to say I was filled with the worries of the evening and my aspirations. I didn't care! I don't!

Only a lone dog in the air, sleek Rotweiler whining and feeding fussily on the white juicy brains stamped in my genetic code. Might as well crash the vestry door, claim the camaraderie of the nameless, embrace the celestial beast whose armor creaks with the thousand spoons of grey porridge left stuck in sleeping mouths. Worm-pus of surrender.

Holy soldiers fucking their cards on the table. The love hand is the only game resembling full speed. Too much happens in my head that I want to live in my life. I am now sending you this disease as my last hook. Nail yourself like Jesus up on it!

Instar (Where the Sun is Born)

Falling asleep staring at a light bulb. The image left on your retina by the light travels with you. Becomes an example of all the rest. Whatever is not here now but was before. A reminder. Perhaps in place of the star which no longer appears. Perhaps the form which never revealed itself as other than the form between this and that. The nascent metaphor with pudgy little arms—baby arms—unable to grasp the tail of the comet. Regardless, you're asleep! And without even realizing it you need to be brave to stay that way. Thought knows that and so too the subconscious with its snapping forceps trying to catch a dream. Only wanting the most succulent but sometimes having to settle for the out-of-practice, repetition, or even the dream-series.

Travelling a long way to the East to find the instant, your personal Orient of a single breath. Your baggage is all the moments of your life packed and arranged in alphabetical order. With a thousand identical black suitcases you front the final barrier. 'Only memories from D to L are permitted on this flight, don't you know anything?', the customs officer roars. Sweating awkwardness, you begin the process of dropping your bundled life down a chute marked 'Not for transferal'. Later, arriving at last in a city of mosques and Chinese billboards, you proceed, naked apart from an umbrella, to join the immense file of pilgrims waiting to enter the temple where the sun is born. There a group of elegant young women in glittering saris pluck you from the crowd. 'You cannot possibly enter this holy place', the women explain. 'You are wearing your skin and its every pore smells offensively of the past.'

My Own Dream (Witnessing)

They have given me my own dream. And a map. I go out to buy things for the race. Friends are to compete against friends. Brother against brother. Looking down at my body I wonder, 'What came first? The necklace, earring, bracelet or ring?' Everything seems heavy and unpredictable. My life-jacket floats around me like a variety of sponge cake. Off to one side of the dream's arena I spot a bunch of people of a certain type who want to deliver the news. Beside them, in a frenzy, is a character from the movie I was watching when I fell asleep last night. Simultaneously this person is you and not you. And because I know you are the witness I turn my back and step into the scented evening. If this is to become some grotesque drama then I shall certainly exercise my authority as a contestant. Do whatever I must. Trade my withdrawal for beads of submission. Eat the walls of buildings.

What to do when even dreams are processed and presold by a thought corporation? Rules endlessly elaborating so we will wear ourselves out-guessing their evolution. And the threat of filming from every angle to keep us at our paranoid best.

I take a tram to a part of the city that has no people. There I can retrain my body into the elegant statements of winter trees with their forked and devious limbs, sparse and absolute under the panning sky. I find a creek that is slowly filling the harbour with silt and am reassured by pelicans wordlessly surviving shit. I don't want graveyards or angels. My face still has no name. I am about to start living my life.

To Remain

What is left (?)

I can barely lift my head
knowing that I will never escape distance.
It is too hard to be human.
To be simple.
A single hair on my head moves, caught
in the fascinating work of draughts.
It is also indifferent, that hair.
You slide your fingers under it as my life disappears
and I hear your contracting heart.
Does it sound like what happens to me?
Does it sound like the mill of the sun
working like a great nerve in the sky?
With your hand there, crumpled,
I welcome the silkworms and all the proven ugliness.
Everything that's relative
becomes sodden with you.
My only purpose is to become lightless
so that you may illuminate this resignation.
But I have a rage hanging
and connecting me to the mass of earth.

    This morning snowfall on Mount Tsuguri. A raw chill in Mariko's hands as she braids my hair. Sadness first, then a hushed shadow on water as if my lover was there, as if he could speak.

    Branches framing a door—
    grey stones swept bare
    eager to grasp bare feet:
    nine months to give birth to stillness.

You have found my samurai journal.

All the lines are blurred.

Like oneself's self.

All writing is implacable.

Writing to forsake the stone.

> All those involved were in love in spring.
>
> By winter their love was ended.
> By the time winter—clairvoyant winter!—stepped up
> to her chilly altar full with certain words of fortune,
> their love was over.

Those who don't have it
know the true nature of fulfilment.

It is the third anniversary of Kotaro's death. I light incense sticks before the photo of him in his new suit on our visit to the Heian Shrine. I open again the scroll of a Chinese poem he gave me. I do not know what to say about his fate: to come here alone so far from all family, to be my first lover, to die at twenty three. I pour two glasses of rice wine—one for him, one I sip.

> *Yet how will you reach the wine?*
> *What did you dream when you died?*
> *That sleep that simply wound forward.*
> *Between sleeping and sleeping you left.*
> *All the wine you did not drink*
> *we will have to drink for you.*
> *Wanting to climb Mount Alishan*
> *you planned a short visit to Taipei,*

then fell asleep and never woke.
In the space of dreams how will you find a path?

Wanting to touch your hand I leave the incense burning. Needing to live, I look away.

. . . on visit to city intolerable sense of panic at Ikebukuro Station. Surely among all these faces is his face, but then my cheeks flinch, confused: am I searching for my lover's face or the face of our unborn son, our child adrift in nowhere.

Overheard in this morning's dream, two women talking: 'The spirits of Kotaro and Chieko will not be Kotaro and Chieko but don't tell her that.' And if there were really no ghosts? If we wake into nothing?

> Stones tumbling and tumbling in the autumn drain.
> Between wall and wall
> the river stands corrected.

Why the anger?

You laughed at my suit.
Saying 'What does that collar make you,
a man or a horse or a dog?'
Then once I was dead you deftly buttoned
at my neck and smoothed my chest
as I had seen you do with rice,
raw under water.

As a child, I was part of China.
The only white boy who was Chinese.
Over and over,
with a tongue like a wooden spatula,
I ran together the words
of Gekkutsu-Sei:
'set down the emerald lamp,
Take it up—exhaustless.
Once lit,
A sister is a sister.'

You are my sister
and so I remained ignorant

of all you ever told me.
(I loved you without needing to know anything.)

Now in this sour agony,
this cold water where I am falling away,
where I am cabbage or something done,
you are my sister-lover.
Bearer of little paper gifts
whispering happy-sad
notes to the dead.

There is no point saying
they have no meaning.
After all, what is the difference
between Japanese and Chinese
death poems.

Five rice dumplings?

Startled awake: in the dream I am walking uphill guided by a woman from the time when people had no names. 'How far is it?' I ask. The woman replies,
'As far as yesterday. As far as two lives.'
... In Seattle visiting my sister. She tells me computers could have been immortal but one computer taught death to the others. Their bodies remain forever because they have no ghosts to let their spirit continue.

In the Imperial Park a goose attacked my dress.
Food and the source of food all the same.
My hand in the bread, the bread: one shimmer of infinite crumbs.

Weighing your hand
it is as heavy as the secret
it does not know but touches.

Today, when all of the city leaves
a bruise, I might let you feel
my presence.

How is this effected?
How do the dead take their place
among the living?

By moving further away.

Putting my arm through yours
and not letting go as I spin into the new
subterranean universe.

Inside the wings of ten thousand
pigeons your eyes flutter shut
on their stone bed.

When the last bird has left
the square the shadow of the flock
remains.

It falls across you as you squat
to retrieve your packet, dropped
when I bit you on the leg.

In your mind is the thought
that our lovemaking had the anticipation
and patience of fossicking.

Automatically your hands flick
over the crumbs, searching for the one
among them.

The one to feed this persistent goose
which now seems to have
no definite form.

Staring you wonder why suddenly
its gooseness seems to be both
uncertain and more certain than ever.

The city becomes another
as two cities
collide.

I pull your dress into the sky . . .

Tear poetry from the poem
you said.

Existence is so godless.

Here, where there are no more departures,
we change the histories and gorge on the destinies
of those who refuse to die.

Where my body once made allowance
for squeezing itself onto paper,
now I understand how indelicate
thought and how futile
any creation that must fight for existence
outside the self.

All that goes beyond
no longer belongs.

This explains why you still belong to me
but I no longer belong to you.

I have been torn from you
and so it is that you now live
within me.

The whole presence of you
seeks.

You think it is for me
but you are really looking for the poetry,
our gold idea.

This morning flying back to Tokyo, to the village, to my mother's small house halfway toward the sky, its garden walled off from the mountain's gaze. I bring paper and fragrances from the cedar country of the Americas to receive the blackened ink my lover once breathed on. But I do not want words—my hands hunger for the sharp precision of gesture. I will draw what happens when the inside of things spills out. I am not the beaker of water but the shattering.

'How appalling to have left this paper-mopuntain behind'.

Then type backwards, delete 'p'.

'How appalling to have left this paper-mountain behind'.

I'm fairly dazed here
– lots of driving today
– and time in secret world
– then alcohol to seem normal
– now have major headache.

This sound like a Chinese poem, perhaps?

Through the wall your sounds carry.
Waxing and waning of the tap.
Spraying rose mist, the tiny wet beads
arousing your skin.

I hear you and I am apprehensive.
Always if not holding you.
How elaborate love gets
before it becomes simple.

The computer squeaks.
Reach out with my fingers.
Then stop.
Enjoy for a moment its powerlessness.
Touch the keys.

'I cause you.'

Through the wall your crying.
You have missed me so long
that your face is not the one
I knew.

'The problem of death
remains.'

Last night I took another lover for the first time. If Kotaro was a ghost or even a presence, a breath stirring a curtain in the house, I would feel guilty. Dawn came slowly. Life flowed.

>Where the flowers reach in darkness
>hold my face to the stars.
>Two candles protect us—
>from the shaken mattress a single feather.

Burning low, the cedarwood incense carries my daughter's gaze to the empty window even the birds don't visit. 'Tell me again about my father', she says. By day my hands have been working the mud for the Bunraku masks that later will shriek on the gallery wall beside the rice bowl and the holder for sticks of appleblossom. Now in the kitchen my hands are blue, trimming gutted fish.

> *Smoke prays all by itself*
> *in the room where the curtains are drawn.*
> *The wound in my right hand*
> *is faithful to your inaccurate knife.*
> *Little one of endless distances,*
> *you arrive before me.*

It's a night of smells.

Fish, which you do not prefer.
The window I do not walk past
opening
into the wine.
Your mirror smelling of cinnamon incense.
And apple yesterday.
Cavities of the body.

Many hours have passed
and a month ago your letter arrived.

I reach into my life
to find it.

I read it to each of your friends
and it helps us to see
the road you sit beside, no doubt
beneath the oblivion
of an escaping sun.

It is night
and the sunlight smells
of all it's trapped in.

The little sticks in your hand remain empty.
Rice
gone cold.

The moon soared and then fell.

To console is never possible.

It is a trick of love.

A shadow of you that moves.

Over a lifetime, the macadamized heart.

But is it no consolation?

No consolation that you live.

Lanterns hang by the river on an auspicious night. By twos and threes the children collect wafer-like candies and balls of sugar. Later at the first elementary school presentation, an honorary guest, I sit, politely smiling, to acknowledge the graduates. In the space between two breaths we carry the secret world to give those we love. It is broken in two, reforms, is broken in two. Tomorrow another small ceremony of loss and expansion: at the tree-lined threshold Michiko leaving for University in the capital.

What binds the living and the dead? Are the dead like children who keep spinning in one spot because the sensation of falling over perpetually surprises them with freshness? Or do they simply look back at us from a world beyond banalities?

> *I live: I let go.*
> *I dream and the dead dream through me.*
> *By the lake where we kissed*
> *flowers have the scent of your wrists*
> *and the waterfowl that drift under clouded skies,*
> *don't they almost remember our faces?*
> *My hands bear the scars I took forever from your forehead.*
> *The butterfly that stumbles at my window*
> *has counted every button I undid*
> *to stroke your chest . . .*

What is death?

All I can do is compare it to you
who were the most full of life
in all my living.

Death conserves mystery
as silk does
with the movement of your legs.

I count it
as I used to count and record
your many different smiles.

And what is left from death
but my soul, what is left over
from the effort of dying.

My soul and you.
It is no compromise that they remain
forever apart.

Chinese-American with unpronounceable name, the one my girlfriends and I nicknamed Kotaro,
how quickly you took my hand the moment I shivered:
how little I know of you beyond your death.

. . . In a dream I check into a hotel called Devastation. It is a love hotel but I am alone. On the walls lurid posters of erotic poses, velvet and fetishes, the soft trickle of couples making love on a discrete TV screen buried in a fish tank. I open the blinds and opposite me across the bay Mt Fuji is steadily erupting, pouring its glowing rivers of lava towards me. The sky crackles with meteor sparks and jagged lightning. It is then I realise I have left Michiko unattended in the bath . . .

Today sunlight protects me from this constant invasion of the past. I work, I prepare sculptures and installations for an exhibition in Nara. My agent rings twice, my daughter once to be sure I am eating sensibly. I lie. Food disgusts me, that obscene activity of the mouth that should kiss without pause forever and forever, or else be filled only with silence . . .

Why stop here?

Shocked that you fell in love
with an ant?

Furtively you prepare my dinner
one year after my death.
No days remain for you the present.
Half of each day is the future
and half is the past.
Making nasturtium salad
you pretend to be me
and imitate yourself.
Remember in that colour
between orange and red
your stained face on the day
I became a nomad.
Dismantle your expression
with the silver paring knife
moulded by some god
of knives.

A temptation of despair interferes
with the time you take
to get the batter just right
as you imagine slitting love
from end to end, gutting
love because nothing
is invisible to the heart
but the heart itself.

Ah, what you always are!

A woman who would open me out
and show me to myself.

All knowledge of me
exists nowhere else.

I do not accept
what you don't.
Even a familiar heresy
is still a heresy.

In Berlin for an exhibition I phone home. My daughter and her new boyfriend are bottling cherries. Drunk on sake I wake up on a barge. The owner, an artist, shows me his mural of shattered glass where the face shreds itself in strips: myself at 20, at 40, at 60 all interspersed. Why are you so beautiful, he asks, and so silent? I smile. He doesn't know when he touches my cheek he is swimming already through the sea that began his life.

> *Almost midnight, the waiter has stacked the chairs on the table.*
> *The glass of green liqueur is still half full.*
> *Your hand goes on holding mine.*
> *Two clocks on the wall with their untranslated time.*
> *The river has found the sea.*

Flow atlas flow.

Our bodies in pieces.

Hand delivered messages.

Memorials of the lung and library air.

How I would have loved to grow grey with passion.

Our history absolute with food and games,
                                          death and dreams.

The part where I was to regret the loss of you
has been stripped.

Everything now is jangly.

It must be some reaper's prank
that you cannot find me
though you travel from city to city,
from estrangement to estrangement.

A pool table is filled with water: a small sea rocking with gentle waves. Kotaro and I lean against a rock wall, kissing. We are both fifteen. We seem to be underground yet also in a pub in Seattle. Our mouths keep kissing and kissing. His fingers slip inside me, moistening me. Later he is on top, my legs clasping him tight. His eyes shine with the tears that outlast time.

    Waking there has been an earth tremor on Mount Tsuguri. The photo of myself dressed up for Coming of Age Day lies on the bedroom floor, its glass cracked. I laugh, then feel his laughter shining suddenly through me. Alone in the house I wonder how my mother is, asleep in the shaded cemetery on the slope of Mount Tsuguri.

The bottom half of a kettle fills up
much slower
than the top half.

Nothing we did
was about believing the other.

The other was all
for us.

Truth was just like affection;
faith as small as the horrifying instant.

You liked tea.
I the larger drunkness.

In the pavilion by the lake my daughter and I drink beer that is very cold. My teeth, always sensitive, ache with each mouthful. Our hosts have driven us here to watch darkness settle on the water. Jungle birds are flittering in a vast enclosure larger than the pavilion, their greens and blues and yellows lit up by the sudden rush of sunset.

'I feel proud of your art but I do not understand it', Michiko says in English for the benefit of our hosts. I do not tell her that I understand nothing myself.

Our hosts have gone back to discussing local painters in Spanish. 'Tomorrow', the Festival organiser says, 'we will take you further up into the mountains—it is, how do you say, the place where clouds are at home among people.'

Your life parries my death.

You say, 'Lovers do love each other
if they are, in
fact, in
love.'

Five years old. My awkward hands trace the three curved lines for 'river'.

Chaos is never annulled by language.

Ever since I have become
unlike anything
I have been trying to tell you
that no evidence
exists.

The paintings that would be there if I wielded a brush in my dreams.

And still you keep preparing
your case.
Proving my slavery
to time.
What I once filled.

Seven years old, my daughter points to the photo of Kotaro, 'I want that one for my daddy.'

'This is a photo of him at the march.'

'We don't know if he ever had mumps.
    His mother cannot speak.'
'Three years ago
    the photograph of the dog
        he took fell from the
            wall and broke
                my toe.'

How special are all the things
with which you fill
the void.

What I now fill.

In Kyoto a cemetery so close to a laundromat and a bath house. Steam to cleanse us of loneliness, snow resting on bamboo.

My forgotten mouth with
telling you that perhaps
what is gone
is gone

but I forgot.

Every strip should be a line that is jagged and clear, but there should also be one line that has the same length as your body, the length of every breath you have yet to draw.

And . . .

there is no beginning in starting
your life over and over
with a dead man.

I am eighteen. You hold my face in your hands. In twelve months time the earth takes your hands.

You should forget.

'Um' is a recognition
that you should.

As I step off the bus, the wind takes the bundle of your new poems and scatters them everyway. Retracing their journey down the street, I gather them in, all but one leaf.

Then you say,
'My desire has a method.
Every want is unique.
Reality is of a mental kind.
My lover may be inconvenient now
that he is dead but
whenever I speak of life
and death these days
it is with unexplicit
language.'

Not *in*.

What you never wrote is it always written?

Can you have a ghost sleeping?
How stale is a million?
What do you know of the alliances between mysteries?
Where do they go, the refusals that are unrefused?
What kind of deal have you made with repetition, what recurs?
Have you imagined the truth of disappearing?
Do apparitions cast a shadow on our creations?
Does love know anything of taking turns?
How alarmed is the moon by mystics gazing upwards?
Might hunger and cold be indispensable to the universe?
Do you imagine the dreams from which we never wake?
Will you perfect our love without me?
Will you know the incomparable?

In the small house below Mount Tsuguri I cut paper and splice photos of fireflies for an installation. The intricate laid out on a bare table of moonlight. Insects I have no name for enter the room. What I hold, what I don't hold mingle their shadows.

At twenty I grasped my face with both hands before the mirror. What to do with this monstrosity, this beauty? Perfection that gives no joy, this cold lake that gives no shelter . . .

In Trinidad for two days I take a taxi to the Taoist temple overlooking the harbour. Someone tells me in the ocean that stretches before me is the exact opposite point on the earth to Mount Alishan. I pose a question to the oracle: 'When will I see the ghost of my dead lover?' Lighting incense and throwing dice, matching numbers and little slips of paper, I receive the reply 'You are not old enough yet.' I wonder, how old do you have to be to see the dead? And when I am dead, will I have lost whatever tied us together?

> *Do sleeping fish climb water-sand mountain?*
> *Do those who fall asleep in the sky become fish?*

At Taichung the University rises tier on tier above the city. My installations hang in a wide room of light. At the presentation I learn of my place in the history of art: my experiments now called 'post-Asia'.

Facing China—almost touchable this night across the straits—transparencies of mist obscure your face, you who were my China. Again two glasses of wine on a table. I reach across to make a toast, am about to say your name, but warplanes (of which country?) ricochet and thunder above me. I imagine my skin shredded, my eyes seared as they shatter, incineration my end-art, and I wonder: how will a man who dies in his sleep understand a woman who dies in fire? How do you say the secret name peace gives itself in the language of screams?

. . . Camping on Alishan with my daughter at 80. Dawn rises in flotillas of white birds. Endlessly the chill world deepens around me. Still no ghost . . .

Secret codes
have given way
to scraps.

From here,
it all looks silly and avoidable.
Here, where
we avoid nothing
because there is nothing to avoid.

Sometimes now
I even find myself considering
our relationship
from a literary point of view.
I study and collect
picture postcards
of you going about your business.

Boiling eggs.

Banging against the pan-metal
like the shuffling of horses
on ancient cobblestones.

On the edge
of your first drawing.
Confident and inaccurate.
Eyes without mouths.
A river-dragon scrawled
beneath a beetle with a broken leg
that crawls incuriously
across your imagination.

And this evening, when the history
of literature continues, tying
your hair in that little scarf,
your teeth shining like ice
in their sockets, courting
yourself with makeup—lip-
gloss, shimmering powder,
even mascara!

Is any love unreasonable?

I know your face
in its new beauty but have
no idea whether you are dressed
as a man or dressed
as a woman.

I have no muscles
with which to move my eyes
or tongue so I beg
'Create me, without inspiration,
in the work of your face.

If you grow knives
kill me first'.

With your tiny nail scissors,
the miniature ones
from the vending machine,
you pare an opening
in the shadow that surrounds you.

Out you flow
like a river winding
in its own evolution.
There is no bad news tonight.
You are surviving.

The Summoning Wound

(Book of Paul Celans & César Vallejos)

Conversation Beyond the Cloudline

Paul:

The river's curling weeds and refuse
are a strange bitterness—
instantly they filled me with the fragrance of distant mountains,
with the unseen purples greens and silvers
that only grow from the world's spine.

My fingers slipped, spinning through ancestral mud,
and some heaviness in the inverted stars
that dwell in dark waters
permitted the crossing of oceans.
With the blurred hearing of the drowned
I navigated long secret tunnels where worlds,
places, broken syllables keep creating
earthspeech.

I woke under bright celestial stars
a Sunday evening, about seven.
A fine drizzle marked signs under my shirt.
Solfegged Latin, blindly stumbling from a church,
was writing the names for the unborn
across the evening air.

I sat outside on a stone bench in the Plaza,
counting the white flowers of the dead that fell towards me.
A group of boys improvised lovesongs on quenas,
a girl sold lemonade and soft tortillas.
The white skyline of mist
had just begun to enter
the jagged alleyways that balance
on the edge of falling forever into night.

A young man already dressed in an old age I would never grow into,
the two of us carrying our own portable time,

placed his finger in the hollow space between the two veins of
	my wrist
where death had quietly begun to blossom,
tenderly he placed his name-place on me:
Santiago de Chuco.

El Cholo (Vallejo):

When you first washed up here
white as a virgin fish
I took one breath and smelt Paris.
Anywhere I would know those cigarettes
and that place in the world that is far.
All those streets I loved to walk,
that ability to immortalize a glass of brandy.
Then my last days at the Clinic Aragó where,
chloroformed into the aether,
I slipped through the gathering cruelty of the sky
and drifted back calmly to earth,
landing (my hair slightly greyed) in Santiago de Chuco,
my hometown.
A letter received in transit
instructed me to take up the still vacant post of Schoolmaster.
Teaching twelve year olds on rainy Thursday afternoons
is a bit of a chore
even when you hold letters of recommendation
from the President of the Republic of the Dead.

Paul:

Me parece que no hay hornos aqui
pero la tierra es una herida abierta.
Pintados de blanco o azul

los muros están rojos de sangre.
¿No es cierto?

El Cholo (Vallejo):

I think it was the wound that summoned us.
These are ancient bones.
If one grasped them
one would grasp why we are here.

Paul:

Eradication is for those who do not want to know.

El Cholo (Vallejo):

Dust to dust
I see you.
There is an afternoon when the singing
goes too long.
Even among the dead
the butterflies cannot choose the sky's colour.

Clothed (César Vallejo)

César—it's three years and you haven't changed your suit: same shirt, coat, buttons, not the tie. On your fingers, that bug of a ring. Same frown. That line, dwarf turned sideways between your yes—most hand some man of lips. Your eyes, simultaneous with the little peaks of your upper mouth. Bone of the brow with the striking density of a horse. *Turning to look*. Licorice-like. A strong sweet. There is no necessity to say fine as the three buttons crawl in the same time, in the same temper that covers the vast smoke-tipped expanse of trees, both up and down your arm. To the brain. To the book. Clothed in you. As the sun picks only some leaves to make flow. Your thumbs translate the whole of the river in to which has been tossed the sticks of time. Your hands uncollect them. It might have been a sneer had your beauty not taken it over. (The *look away* from the book never put down.) Handkerchief glowing from your forehead. And how your heart points towards that shadow that comes from all directions. Looking out over your heart you notice us. How we haven't changed despite eternity which opened with the double breast. The ocean shivers and in your elbow's folds the desert sands go on with the songs that lure all men away from water.

OPEN THE CHINESE FAN, PAUL CELAN
On remembering our mothers.

How many instants in the fan. While in fact, crimson, wet, the conversation soaked in breath overcomes the pans that seek their balance. Bearth shines? Was it justness in your hand or stars at the tips of the digits? Sitting, watching, the weighing of the gold, eyes hidden behind white, white paper of rice, the glint arches inwards, bright frost of soul, slipping past the wad of words you stuff between yourself and the void. In this peace, the moment of the wrist that flicks, terror looks like all fear, the self-created breeze so slight. Hah! In what perpetual night they count as you number cherry blossoms in the spread palm. This is stigmata. A piece of paper that crushes. And what unfolds is always death, the perfect scene. *Remember them. As if, as if* . . . nothing was ever sold. How possible, betrayal. How capable you were of suffering.

César Vallejo's Handshake

Dead these sixty years in Paris
where rain and snow once more
bury the hungry boulevards,
you stand head bowed
above what seems to be a gravestone,
the wide hat of a ranchero in your hand
and with the grimace of a man who loses all in a cockfight.
Amigo,
I hear the shrill song that flows under your breath.
In darkest nightmare summoning the names of all colours
you mutter so quietly
the savage diction of a cerebral chemist.

Or I meet you in the hospital
where polishers whirr
enormous circles on the moonlit floor.
The X-rays tacked up on the wall,
their dark scrawl
threading the pain of the earth to the pain of the stars.
A white bird drops by saying 'Open this door.'
The curtain of your sickbed waits to move
like the sail of a ship.
In Peru the horse of your childhood
still chews its grass, tosses its mane
in the last dryness of summer.
A poem or a life
ripples between such trivial and such portentous matter,
incorporates derision,
dispenses its own handshakes.

And if after so many words
not one word.
And if among so many breaths
not one sigh
crosses the vacuum.

In a dream you woke to find the windowsill opposite your bed
lined with money,
little gold and silver coins that shone at you.
In the next room the same
and at the front door
a row of coins the same.

Such embarrassing gifts among bandaged heads.
Bloom of putrefaction on the skin
of the one who guards twilight.
Graced always with the wealth of the air,
César Vallejo,
under Paris rain
seeking the correct and final gesture,
giving these aesthetic otherworldly objects
their human name.

Undrowned

When he emerges from the water, Paul's hair is dry. Like the steam of plants, all his moisture radiates from within. It comes off him in 'I believe' 'I believe'. He laughs, transporting the sauce from life to death and back. The land might be too dry, but life's too good. He thinks, *this is the first time you need to know.* The little puddles of foot he leaves in his wake are largely undefined yet feet. He slides over the mountain and holds earth to earth with each step. On other days, which seemed so important, all his skin had been stripped to build yet another nest. Now the clean water deep in his heart refracts light from all that is broken as if it is an error cherished after the most brief of exposures. He emerges from deep within the quiet dangerous motion knowing you have to love your country to write about why you hate it. All the shallows flow past without touching him. The sun on his face feels like his mother's most immediate answer. And what was the question? Just a little cloud which like water out of water looked for somewhere to fly. All the little tears come after.

César, Well-Dweller

Waterladen and lifted to heaven,
the eyes still glitter
on their journey.
The last teeth have fallen off
and the cheekbones like the milk of darkness
have spread their film
across the water's surface.

Beyond the unsteady meniscus
all is roots
and the immense tangle of other lives.
Be content with your small death.
The compact earth
has no other face
to offer the sky.

The Severed Head

In primal innocence
alone before what-is-not
a head singing.

The head sees the world. Its speaking overwhelms it.

Two heads, severed, stand alone before God. They do not want biography to cloud the issue.

Lamenting is ancient, like the lover whose eyes were burnt out. Lamenting when the ground you stand on is stripped away: being a voice with no body.

A little winding path to two shoes and a rock. The head, not yet severed, is walking it. The naming of the dark has not started yet. Words, stored like small beads, are placed in the back of the forehead. Later, when only the singing is left, they initiate a constellation.

Witnessing without dabbling in private details means witnessing to what might be anyone.

Orpheus lost the wife who was his soul. He regained her through his singing only to lose her again. Carelessness, or a sign that poetically to speak is always to be the one who has lost rights. Even to himself. Even to the smallest portion of happiness.

To speak out of a fate. To transcend that fate.

For all the frenzy of the maenads Orpheus' head bears no resemblance to a 20th Century head. No part of the brain has been cut away and there is no evidence of any surgical procedure.

In the river the floating head
the part cut away, the part still singing.

The head summons. The head is a wound. How does a wound summon? To dwell in a wound, to speak from a wound is to live without defenses like a lover.

Wounds we have no name for require singing.

The lover knows how a face in its tenderness goes back beyond many lives. The wound we have no name for, the wound in the palm of the hand that goes back beyond many lives, links us to a terrifying heaven we have yet to invent.

Two worn heads in a cupboard singing in unison or chiming slightly off key like damaged gongs, two worn heads singing in a bleakly damaged landscape of the 21st century. Why do they both speak of the peculiar guilt of existing at all, of their presence on earth being perhaps only to rob another of his cup of coffee? What it means to be innocent with both eyes open. And still to sing.

Travelling into distant lands, the head may seem exotica, a weirdness-speaker. Yet it remains here, persistently among us. How familiar its babble, what might be ourselves peeled back, the landscape without the lie of the land.

Severed, a head talks for the headless. When it sings it seeks the right pitch to rebuild the world.

Paul Celan and the Pointless

Well, Paul Celan, how do they write what is real? Your wife's dreams are stabbing you. The Buddhist has a monotonous voice. The Buddhist is a prizewinner in a world where the spit of the mouth is poetry. Arrive in Japan, Paul Celan. Find the Master. Walk into the river and study death as if the jar was full of silt. We should all dive into darkness, against our own ideas, against our will and what we thought was the way. And did you find water? The sun pours itself into a blue glass. Conscious, we are still and still the world. The world. Water. Grace. And you with your little white fence around the dead! Your greatest joy was the story with no point, the koan, your arm a sentence of ash that fell lightly and with grace to our ears. But, Paul Celan, you never reconciled the fire with what might put it out. In what monster's path we found you, sitting and conversing with mystery, face turned away from its face, meeting what you did not know as if finding yourself finally within yourself. You are the way only your creator would understand it, the break of every wave saving itself to crash unalterably in your heart. Does the place of thinking shift in darkness and in silence? Paul Celan, the pointless.

Vallejo's Jacket

General and mark of the sea.
Background and burned.
There, hanging, the balancing act
in something which reminds his shoulders
to swing.
Amputating one arm from the other
   and the abecedarian
      from spelling.
Even inside the dead, his jacket,
supplementarily good and thought about.
Far from the corollary
   and the tide-gate which stopped
      their hands.
For Vallejo's jacket is the half
   in its boiling state, what might
      put an end to
the blooming and blowing and blushing.
No more will go astray!
He who seeks a movable grave in its arms
   will fool the buffoon.
And especially this comb and tuft
   will rattle and snap.
For nothing every condition.
Every bent form at the foot of certain ideas.
Loose animal casing on the outer!
There is a giant application to supply
   with response.
Are these your people?
Are the juices from the gravalaxy
   covering your accelerating sleeves?

Paul Celan Stepping Out

He walked out of Bucharest.
He left Vienna.
He walked away from his legs
from childhood
from the heavy drift of apple blossom
the soliloquy of ash.
He stepped out of his clothing
his familiar name, his first voice.
He left Sarajevo Prague Split Venice.
He left his watch his right arm
his trachea
and the best part
of his impatiently talking toes.
Rinsed clean of time and doorways
he stepped beyond his shoes his underwear his death
and saying farewell to the hairs of the riverbank
to the smooth skin of conscripted molecules
he entered the waters of the Seine
where he built his home—
a space that shines with lost words,
mouth that drinks the sky,
autumnal tree blossoming within its death,
sap dying from blossoms.

The Poet, Vallejo, Announcer of Movement

Remember the source of Vallejo's manied confidence, his centipede fear of clocks.

He knew the slight heaviness of debts (they sink they float they travel midway). The splosh in the cabinet was his water poem; in the sky, windy June, his sky poem; the whole earth . . . his overcoat.

The moon creeping around looking for its fatness sniffing at Vallejo's wordy footprints was his unfound metaphor and one blue and two blues his non-identical twin colours for colouring with a tinge the annoying little tongue of the girl who would seal his poems with her lips. He counted me before following his soul onto the hopscotch squares of the solids.

I said with his left pages *Listen with all 70 deluded Peruvian eardrums* and when finding the final dynamite poem of acts and corporeal stupefaction *Do you believe his body*?! Remember Vallejo's gods hanging from the lifted foot,

sole black and cracked his unsounded fizz and splutter: *By cutting a star the day saves its eyebrows. The hieroglyphs, by night, set free the new movements.*

Conversation at the Juncture of the Napo and the Ucuyali Rivers, Amazonas

Paul:

At the confluence of waters
words return.
It was the meeting of waters that drew me here.
Reluctantly, at El Cholo's suggestion,
I set out—
one further journey to break the second death
imprisoning voice.

El perro invisible (Li Po):

I have dwelt here in calm for some time.
A thousand years, a few hours sleep are much the same.
Once through my spirit self, green water frog,
I advised the shaman
on suitable tactics to use against the Spaniards—
an hour ago, five hundred years.
My crafted Chinese speech
curves through air
and echoes strangely round me
as all languages.
I have listened to my poems in the words of tree frogs
and in the sky's gesture of bird swarms—
in that speech most of all I see hope.

Paul:

And the people, those who lived here,
did you save them? Are they around us?

El perro invisible (Li Po):

Sometimes I see their ghosts, not often.
They have not lingered as you and I have lingered.
The earth asks further duties of us:
speech must matter.

Paul:

Calm one of huts and drinking songs,
friendship's smoke edging over
mountain-rippled valleys,

you
stillness-maker,
drunken brother of stumblings,

your speech, all its measured sounds,
gone under, sealed in final water,
this excess speech of the wordless,

your pawmarks
give you eternity.

Postscript: Elizabeth Bishop finds a wasps' nest in an abandoned building inscribed with a poem by Li Po, Ouro Preto, 1965.

Dawn:
this wide passageway of ghosts.

OBJECTS OF YOU IN WATER

Spoon

The river has changed its name
though the two banks sit eyeing each other,
the row of blank totem stones
reflected back and forth
in the vanishing that joins them.
Incident number one: a drawing of a spoon
floated by before snagging on an overhanging root
of willow exposed by the land's
deathward leap. Always
your face in the sky
etched by itinerant leaves
and that wistful passion of just seeing you
in the ordinary blaze of things—
one more step along a journey home.

Chandelier Drop

We don't talk of crystal balls anymore
but in one is where I imagined you.
Why are words so cute you hang them in your room for hours?
Why are flies more austere than monoliths?
Why do you enter my mouth like a wasp
to set fake aphorisms buzzing?

Who twisted us around so we can never move in the one story,
our histories all wrong, and set us both down
maimed and beautiful
exactly right?

Saucepan

Sometimes I see you held inside a cradlesong
but then you are already cradling a saucepan
or setting off across muddy streets,
your hiking boots filled with purpose…

Or is it you, at the door, with a new smile,
your hands filled with coriander root,
a recipe?

You left your old life aboard a boat
on a river of domesticity—
what an odd thing to break my heart,
such erotic bravery.

Bowl and Ice

Later, from distraction, your thumb
with its small cushion of flesh untipped
by the serrated knife, immersed
in a bowl of ice and you laugh drinking wine
above the sea turning to blood
as I continue to cut.

In the tree beyond the kitchen window,
the shadow of its small inhabitant
soundless and drawing us
into the dark.

Bridge

It's a technical term, though no less poetic for that,
not these words, but the one not here,
the bird that flew from the post
in the direction of its older suitor, the earth.
Incident two or three is forgotten.
Number four has to do with you looking away,
towards what I thought was a bird on a railway bridge
but I watched all day and it didn't fly.
You shook compassion into the sky from a cloth you held
between your freezing fingers.
For you, the small figure of the eagle
disappeared through the metal arch
as the train passed beneath it,
solid and holy before the seven-branched tracks.
Which way will we go today?

Portable Roadway

All that the sea can mean—
the place we are going to.
What use there is fire?
The sunlight was all inside us,
all our food gone on offerings
the gods never eat.

The sky was closed down
so you brought the road with you—
the one line from your mouth to the horizon coming apart—
distance stinging your tongue with words unrecallable as days,
tomorrow and yesterday opening their lips to the tithe,
imitating your littoral cry.

WATER-JUG

I sat on the verandah where the sky was drifting in,
the lines of small white flocks—the dead coming back
the way they had always threatened to.
The large water-jug, at least one hundred years old,
becomes part of my hand—raised over the roof
where the poor live—passionless,
intent on my own mouth.
Momentarily
I am the watcher in a lighthouse.
There is the ship, surrounded by the birds of the dead.
It is full of reports. Of cups for this falling water.

CEILING FOR BALCONY

Incident number six:
pulled the balcony ceiling down and forced all the juveniles to fly or fall.
Today the sky is in my blood.
Were you already married to that galaxy when we met?
You moved so fast I couldn't tell.

Lips

I was frightened when I first saw you changing, your face
unravelling into pain that was also anger and also
all emotion shutting down.
Like the pigeons you murdered,
bits of other lives fluttered screaming
stuck onto your face.
It was like making love but in reverse—
your eyes dilated with otherness,
your lips that didn't move:
'You know, none of us are here.'

Ladle

Coffee and curry steam in the same kitchen,
their hindu-hispanic fragrance
staining the dull air—
a night garden where the trees
split themselves open.
It's always serious,
the town you grew up in.
Those who are taken away.
Those who stay as if the present was a longer place
than anywhere else.
Myself—the self that relinquishes all at night
to the night—I never left this city,
slightly travelling nowhere—to the world
and then on great wings to the brief land of autobiography.
It has as little room to roam in as love.
Everyone there is pressed unbearably
against themselves
and when they try to build other-ships
the world sinks from the weight
of their tools.
It was when I bent to retrieve my hammer
that I first saw your face, your hand
with a ladle
of different glass.

Unnamed Object

The ninth incident came after several undiscussable
because our lovemaking we kept
quite private.
It was short and sharp.
You said,
I am never going to feel your pain.

Sea Bird Eaten by Ants

Who knows when these scattered feathers
adjourned from the sky.

The carcass of a white sea bird
offers sand that will be hard-won
to the loose waves of low-tide.

An ant, I remember, tickles the flesh
of your hand.

Between its jaws a whole other world
crashes through
the lit universe.

Needle

I unstitch words from your arm.
Your eyes smoulder with fire and hurt.
The leaves have coloured your eyes
with the day I was trying to find.
The wind in my garden
and the soft start of rain
make me think of you.
If you come back into the world
I will let go of my pain.

Umbilical Cord

The least of you goes on
        holding tight to the world,
circling like the long arm of a monster trapped in the pool—
longing has no part in these assessments.
Three years since our breaking
the ice preserves a strange nudity of lost flesh,
some sharp butchered instinct that walks away
and still carries
the listless name of earth.

Marker Buoys

Simply a pen scratching on a page
or rats feeding in a disused warehouse—
my journey to you
from this long night of the illuminated kitchen
drifting out to sea in the darkness of space.
When I lost that sense of you speaking from inside me
I felt I had swum a first mile
out into the strong black current
that cuts below each shoreline.

Urn

Where is the thirteenth ocean?
This unlucky number is mine.
I count it with memories, dumbness, your hands
that I see in every one of life's images:
a boy rubbing his head into the back of a man's neck;
so many different jasmines, wildful,
pretending delicacy for the swallows, the ashes.
The urn falls through the floor at midday:
Whom you all love is fortune,
                    is love.

Drifting, Assorted

The marina moored against the grey ache of summer,
this slow lapping
where all the sky banks up.
Objects of you in water:
the ankle or the eye
the shoelace the boating pole the cup and saucer
and the soap rinsed off your hands
in a sink of darkness
where the moon sifts the rice:
all held in a transparent world
where I could name you
and bless
our vanishing.

Sketching Pad

The river wound its way back from the future
to its own mouth.
Still the stones lay, still they erected themselves
                                      in silence.
You drew me in the forest once.
My face in the leaves as if it could fall away from everything
just as easily.
In the scratched lines of your pencil
I was to be the wound opened in remembrance.
All incidents shed in words.

www.ingramcontent.com/pod-product-compliance
Lightning Source LLC
Chambersburg PA
CBHW021327190426

43193CB00039B/334